Our Favorite Pets

Crazy About Birds

Harold Morris

TABLE OF CONTENTS

A Crabtree Seedlings Book

CRABTREE Publishing Company
www.crabtreebooks.com

Birds

All birds have feathers, beaks, and wings.

FEATHERED FACT

Birds come in all sizes and colors!

Choosing the right kind of **pet** bird is important.

zebra finches

FEATHERED FACT

Zebra **finches** are small and quiet. Macaws are large and loud!

macaw

Some birds need more **attention** than others.

FEATHERED FACT

Most canaries do not like to be held.

FEATHERED FACT

Parrots need lots of attention.

Make sure your bird's cage is large enough.

The cage must be kept clean.

FEATHERED FACT

Food and water dishes and all toys should be kept clean too.

Feed your bird good-**quality** food from the pet store.

FEATHERED FACT

There are different kinds of bird food. Find out which one is best for your pet.

Feed your bird fruits and vegetables too!

FEATHERED FACT

Your bird needs fresh, clean water every day.

Like us, pet birds need exercise.

FEATHERED FACT

Your bird will be happier if you **release** it from its cage often.

Only release your bird in a safe room in your house.

FEATHERED FACT

Most birds like to play with toys.

FEATHERED FACT

You can teach some birds to speak or do tricks.

Do not frighten your bird. Speak in a soft voice and do not make sudden movements.

Glossary

attention (uh-TEN-shuhn): Giving your bird attention means spending time with it and making sure it has what it needs.

finches (FINCH-iz): Finches are small birds with short, strong beaks. There are many kinds of finches; a zebra finch is one kind of finch.

parrots (PA-ruhts): Parrots are tropical birds with curved beaks. Some have bright, colorful feathers. There are many kinds of parrots; a macaw is one kind of parrot.

pet (PET): A pet is a tame animal that people keep and take care of for pleasure.

quality (KWAHL-uh-tee): Quality is a measure of how good or bad something is.

release (ri-LEESS): To release something is to set it free.

Index

School-to-Home Support for Caregivers and Teachers

This book helps children grow by letting them practice reading. Here are a few guiding questions to help the reader build his or her comprehension skills. Possible answers appear here in red.

Before Reading

- **What do I think this book is about?** I think this book is about having a bird as a family pet. I think this book is about the funny things a pet bird does.
- **What do I want to learn about this topic?** I want to learn more about taking care of a pet bird. I want to learn how to teach a pet bird to do tricks.

During Reading

- **I wonder why...** I wonder why most canaries do not like to be held. I wonder why parrots need lots of attention.
- **What have I learned so far?** I have learned that pet birds like fruits and vegetables. I have learned that pet birds need clean water every day.

After Reading

- **What details did I learn about this topic?** I have learned that a pet bird's cage needs to be kept clean. I have learned that even the toys of a pet bird should be kept clean.
- **Read the book again and look for the glossary words.** I see the word *parrots* on page 7, and the word *quality* on page 12. The other glossary words are found on pages 22 and 23.

Library and Archives Canada Cataloguing in Publication

CIP available at Library and Archives Canada

Library of Congress Cataloging-in-Publication Data

CIP available at Library of Congress

Crabtree Publishing Company
www.crabtreebooks.com 1–800–387–7650

Print book version produced jointly with Blue Door Education in 2022

PHOTO CREDITS:
Cover photo © Dmitry Pichugin; background illustration on cover and throughout book © Ivanna-Ivashka; Pages 2-3 © cynoclub; Page 4 © OlVic; Page 5 © David Havel; Page 6 © Ajramadhan; Page 7 © Alena Ozerova; Pages 8-9 © Chittiphatra Chanchuang; Page 10 © victoras; Page 11 © frantic00; Page 12 © Stefan von Ameln; Page 13 © Neirfy; Page 14 © Kolotygin Igor; Page 15 © S Wizard; Pages 16-17 and 18 © Christine Bird; Page 19 © Korneeva Kristina; Page 20 © Eppersimons; Page 21 © Santhosh Varghese
All photos from Shutterstock.com

Written by: Harold Morris

Print coordinator: Katherine Berti

Printed in Canada/062022/CPC20220602

Published in the United States
Crabtree Publishing
347 Fifth Ave.
Suite 1402-145
New York, NY 10016

Published in Canada
Crabtree Publishing
616 Welland Ave.
St. Catharines, Ontario
L2M 5V6